Predestination

The Lutheran Difference Series

Thomas Manteufel

with contributions by

Edward Engelbrecht

CONCORDIA PUBLISHING HOUSE · SAINT LOUIS

Written by Thomas Manteufel

Edited by Edward Engelbrecht

All Scripture quotations are from the HOLY BIBLE, NEW INTERNATIONAL VERSION®. NIV®. Copyright © 1973, 1978, 1984 by the International Bible Society. Used by permission of Zondervan Publishing House. All rights reserved.

This publication may be available in braille, in large print, or on cassette tape for the visually impaired. Write to Library for the Blind, 1333 S. Kirkwood Road, St. Louis, MO 63122-7295; call 1-800-433-3954, ext. 1322; or e-mail to *blind.library@lcms.org.*

The Lutheran Confessions quotes are taken from *Concordia Triglotta,* © 1921 CPH

Manufactured in the United States of America

1 2 3 4 5 6 7 8 9 10   12 11 10 09 08 07 06 05 04 03

Contents

About This Series

"Don't you believe that God has a plan for your life? a destiny?"

"Yes. But I also believe that God gives me freedom to make choices."

"How can both of these things be true? Your faith seems so inconsistent."

As Lutherans interact with other Christians, they often find themselves struggling to explain their beliefs and practices. Although many Lutherans have learned the "what" of the doctrines of the church, they do not always have a full scriptural foundation to share the "why." When confronted with different doctrines, they cannot clearly state their faith, much less understand the differences between denominations.

Because of insecurities about explaining particular doctrines or practices, some Lutherans may avoid opportunities to share what they have learned from Christ and His Word. The Lutheran Difference Bible study series will identify how Lutherans differ from other Christians and demonstrate from the Bible why Lutherans differ. These studies will prepare Lutherans to share their faith and help non-Lutherans understand the Lutheran difference.

Student Introduction

This doctrine affords glorious consolation under the cross and amid temptations, namely, that God in His counsel, before the time of the world, determined and decreed that He would assist us in all distresses, grant patience, give consolation, excite hope, and produce such an outcome as would contribute to our salvation.

—Formula of Concord, Thorough Declaration, "Of God's Eternal Election," XI 48.

This is the claim set forth by the founders of the Lutheran church over 425 years ago concerning the biblical doctrine of predestination. Other Christians, and at times some dissenting Lutherans, have not approached the subject of predestination with the same sense of consolation. In fact, many Christians would rather avoid the subject completely.

Traditional Lutherans like to say that the doctrine of predestination is a final examination for a theologian, testing his general commitment to Christian doctrine. The questions in this final exam would read something like the following:

Isn't it arrogant or presumptuous to claim that God has chosen you?

Can anyone ever really be sure?

Should a person accept everything taught by Scripture about this subject simply because it is taught there?

Can this Lutheran doctrine be proved from Scripture?

Isn't predestination a form of fatalism?

Do Lutherans agree with the teaching that God has predestinated some to eternal life and therefore must have predestinated the rest to damnation?

Does predestination ignore human responsibility for repenting and believing in Christ?

Did God choose people to salvation because of what He foresaw they would do?

Did God choose people on the basis of the faith He foreknew they would have?

This study will give attention to these points and help you learn what the Bible teaches and what it does not teach. As you study, pray for God's wisdom and remember St. Paul's words in Romans, "Oh, the depth of the riches of the wisdom and knowledge of God! How un-searchable His judgments, and His paths beyond tracing out! 'Who has known the mind of the Lord? Or who has been His counselor? Who has ever given to God, that God should repay him?' For from Him and through Him and to Him are all things. To Him be the glory forever! Amen" (11:33–36).

An Overview of Christian Denominations

The following outline of Christian history will help you understand where the different denominations come from and how they are related to one another. Use this outline in connection with the "Comparisons" sections found throughout the study. Statements of belief for the different churches were drawn from their official confessional writings.

The Great Schism

Eastern Orthodox: On July 16, 1054, Cardinal Humbert entered the Cathedral of the Holy Wisdom in Constantinople just before the worship service. He stepped to the altar and left a letter condemning Michael Cerularius, patriarch of Constantinople. Cerularius responded by condemning the letter and its authors. In that moment, Christian churches of the East and West were severed from one another. Their disagreements centered on what bread could be used in the Lord's Supper and the addition of the *filioque* statement to the Nicene Creed.

The Reformation

Lutheran: On June 15, 1520, Pope Leo X wrote a letter condemning Dr. Martin Luther for his Ninety-five Theses. Luther's theses had challenged the sale of indulgences, a fund-raising effort to pay for the building of St. Peter's Cathedral in Rome. The letter charged Luther with heresy and threatened to excommunicate him if he did not retract his writings within 60 days. Luther replied by publicly burning the letter. Leo excommunicated him on January 3, and he condemned all who agreed with Luther or supported his cause.

Reformed: In 1522 the preaching of Ulrich Zwingli in Zurich, Switzerland, convinced people to break their traditional Lenten fast. Also, Zwingli preached that priests should be allowed to marry. When local friars challenged these departures from medieval church practice, the Zurich Council supported Zwingli and agreed that the Bible should guide Christian doctrine and practice. Churches of this Reformed tradition include Presbyterians and Episcopalians.

Anabaptist: In January 1525 Conrad Grebel, a follower of Ulrich Zwingli, rebaptized Georg Blaurock. Blaurock began rebaptizing others and founded the Swiss Brethren. Their insistence on adult, believers' Baptism distinguished them from other churches of the Reformation. Anabaptists attracted social extremists who advocated violence in the cause of Christ, complete pacifism, or communal living. Mennonites, Brethren, and Amish churches descend from this movement.

The Counter Reformation

Roman Catholic: When people call the medieval church "Roman Catholic," they make a common historical mistake. Roman Catholicism emerged after the Reformation. As early as 1518 Luther and other reformers had appealed to the pope and requested a council to settle the issue of indulgences. Their requests were hindered or denied for a variety of theological and political reasons. Finally on December 13, 1545, 34 leaders from churches that opposed the Reformation gathered at the invitation of Pope Paul III. They began the Council of Trent (1545–63), which established the doctrine and practice of Roman Catholicism.

Post-Reformation Movements

Baptist: In 1608 or 1609 John Smyth, a former pastor of the Church of England, baptized himself by pouring water over his head. He formed a congregation of English Separatists in Holland who opposed the rule of bishops and infant Baptism. This marked the start of the English Baptist churches, which remain divided doctrinally over the theology of John Calvin (Particular Baptists) and Jacob Arminius (General Baptists). In the 1800s the Restoration Movement of Alexander Campbell, a former Presbyterian minister, adopted many Baptist teachings. These churches include the Disciples of Christ (Christian Churches) and the Churches of Christ.

Wesleyan: In 1729 John and Charles Wesley gathered with three other men to study the Scripture, receive Communion, and discipline one another according to the "method" laid down in the Bible. Later, John Wesley's preaching caused religious revivals in England and

America. Methodists, Wesleyans, Nazarenes, and Pentecostals form the Wesleyan family of churches.

Liberal: In 1799 Friedrich Schleiermacher published *Addresses on Religion* in an attempt to make Christianity appealing to people influenced by rationalism. He argued that religion is not a body of doctrines, provable truths, or a system of ethics but belongs to the realm of feelings. His ideas did not form a new denomination but deeply influenced Christian thinking. Denominations most thoroughly affected by liberalism are the United Church of Christ, Disciples of Christ, and Unitarianism.

Lutheran Facts

All who worship the Holy Trinity and trust in Jesus Christ for the forgiveness of sins are regarded by Lutherans as fellow Christians, despite denominational differences.

Lutheran churches first described themselves as *evangelische,* or evangelical, churches. Opponents of these churches called them "Lutheran" after Dr. Martin Luther, the sixteenth-century-German church reformer.

Lutherans are not disciples of Dr. Martin Luther but disciples of Jesus Christ. They proudly accept the name Lutheran because they agree with Dr. Luther's teaching from the Bible, as summarized in Luther's Small Catechism.

One of Luther's most important writings was *The Bondage of the Will,* which overturned many misconceptions about predestination.

A common closing found in letters by Lutheran pastors has been "D. V." *(deo volente),* which means "God willing." This note reminds both the writer and the recipient that the future is in God's hands.

Lutherans believe people can be sure they will go to heaven because of the sure promise of salvation God gives through Jesus Christ.

Lutherans hold that in the New Testament the church is the "chosen people." They do not support the idea that the Jewish people today or the modern nation of Israel have a special relationship with God as Israel did during the Old Testament.

Three popular Lutheran hymns that mention God's election or choice are "Baptized into Your Name Most Holy"; "A Mighty Fortress Is Our God"; and "Alleluia! Let Praises Ring."

To prepare for "Chosen from Eternity," read Ephesians 1:3–14.

Chosen from Eternity

From eternity, O God,
In Thy Son Thou didst elect me;
Therefore, Father, on life's road
Graciously to heav'n direct me;
Send to me Thy Holy Spirit
That His gifts I may inherit.

—*The Lutheran Hymnal* 411:1

This hymn stanza expresses a belief important to Lutherans. But the idea often is not well understood, even by Lutherans. It has at times led to confusion and disputes. In order that you might receive its intended comfort and help, begin this study with prayer for God's guidance.

1. Sometimes this doctrine is called *election,* and sometimes it is called *predestination.* Do these words mean the same thing, or do they point to different aspects of God's action?

2. Have you ever heard people arguing about this topic? Why do some find it disturbing or offensive? Do you have questions of your own about it?

Chosen

3. The Bible refers to various acts of election (or choosing) by God. In these examples what attitude on God's part is shown in such acts of choosing? Read Deuteronomy 7:6–8; Acts 9:15; Luke 6:13; 23:35; 1 Peter 1:19–20; 2:4, 9; Colossians 3:12; James 2:5; and 1 Corinthians 1:28–29.

11

4. Ephesians 1:3–14 and the other passages in these lessons speak of God's election of those who are saved. According to verses 4–5, what two intended purposes did God have in mind in this election?

5. See Galatians 3:26–28. Since election leads to adoption for "sonship," does it involve only persons of the male sex?

6. Read Ephesians 1:4. When did this divine election take place?

7. Focus carefully on Ephesians 1:4–8. What reasons moved God to choose the elect persons?

8. How do the Second and Third Persons of the Holy Trinity carry out the Father's decision of election, as described in Ephesians 1:3–14? See also 1 Corinthians 12:3 and Acts 13:48.

9. The word translated "praise be" in Ephesians 1:3 is a form of the same Greek word translated "blessed" in the same verse. Blessings are invocations of well-being and good things, pronouncements of well-wishing. Who speaks these blessings in this passage?

Chosen to What?

10. If Christians take Ephesians 1:3–14 seriously, what results of predestination may they expect and look for in their lives?

11. If human beings are expected to use free will to decide to believe in the Gospel in order to have salvation, why did Paul tell the Ephesian believers that they were predestined to be saved? Look at what Paul went on to say in Ephesians 2:1.

12. An acquaintance says to you, "I don't think salvation is just a matter of being predestined. If you tell people that, they will get lazy in their spiritual life, and they will believe there is no need to live good lives and think and act like true Christians. Isn't it better to say: 'God has made it possible for you to be saved, but in the end it's up to you to go on the right path?' " Do you agree? Why or why not?

13. Does the teaching of a predestined salvation contradict the truth that sinners are saved by the merits of Jesus Christ, through faith in Him as the Redeemer?

14. Fatalism involves the belief that every event is governed by an impersonal fate, or perhaps spirits that have no sympathy with people and their problems. Some think that the doctrine of predestination is a form of this belief. Reflect on this comparison.

15. Reflect on the following opinion: Since predestination and election are so hard to understand and so easily applied in a wrong way, would it not be better to ignore the matter and devote time and thought to more important questions of the Christian life?

Blessed!

16. Describe the apostle Paul's emotional response, which breaks forth with praise in Ephesians 1:3, 6, 14.

17. How might these passages influence prayer and worship in your personal life? in your congregation?

Comparisons

All major religions and philosophies wrestle with issues of God's will, human freedom, and the future. Based on the Scriptures, predestination, or election, is taught by most Christian churches. Differences in these teachings will be clarified in later comparisons.

Eastern Orthodox: "With what design did God create man? With this, that he should know God, love, and glorify him, and so be happy forever. Has not that will of God, by which man is designed for eternal happiness, its own proper name in theology? It is called *predestination* of God" (*The Longer Catechism of the Eastern Church*, questions 120–21).

Lutheran: "But the Word of God leads us to Christ, who is the Book of Life, in whom all are written and elected that are to be saved in eternity, as it is written Ephesians 1:4: *He hath chosen us in Him [Christ] before the foundation of the world*" (The Formula of Concord, Epitome XI 6).

Reformed and Particular Baptist: "By the decrees of God, for the manifestation of his glory, some men and angels are predestined unto everlasting life, and others foreordained to everlasting death" (*The Westminster Confession of Faith*, chapter III.III).

Anabaptist: "Concerning the restoration of the first man and his posterity we confess and believe, that God, notwithstanding their fall, transgression, and sin, and their utter inability, was nevertheless not willing to cast them off entirely, or to let them be forever lost; but that He called them again to Him, comforted them, and showed them that with Him there was yet a means for their reconciliation, namely, the immaculate Lamb, the Son of God, who had been foreordained thereto before the foundation of the world, and was promised them while they were yet in Paradise, for consolation, redemption, and salvation, for themselves as well as for their posterity" (*The Dordrecht Confession*, article III).

Roman Catholic: According to the *Catechism of the Catholic Church*, the perfectly purified elect can go directly to heaven when they die (para. 1023). The imperfect elect must spend time in purgatory (para. 1031).

Free-Will Baptist and Wesleyan: "Salvation is rendered equally possible to all; and if any fail of eternal life, the fault is wholly their own" (*Confession of the Free-Will Baptists*, chapter 8).

Liberal: "In the place of the older kind of 'assurance,' which declared that God's absolute word had been proclaimed to us in final form, we must develop a type of assurance which looks confidently toward the establishment of truer dynamic relationships with God through the practical experience of using the best conceptions we have, while striving always for better ones if these are to be found" (G. B. Smith, *A Guide to the Study of the Christian Religion*, p. 550). In other words, Christians cannot know with certainty about the doctrine of predestination and other doctrines because they cannot be sure that Scripture is reliable.

Point to Remember

He chose us in Him [Christ] before the creation of the world to be holy and blameless in His sight. Ephesians 1:4

To prepare for "For Jesus' Sake," read 1 Peter 1:1–12.

For Jesus' Sake

You shall and you shan't—
You will and you won't—
And you will be damned if you do—
And you will be damned if you don't.

—Lorenzo Dow, *On the Doctrine of Particular Election* (1836).

This rhyme is often quoted as a criticism of the teaching of particular election (the idea that only a certain number of people are predestined to be saved). The complaint is that this teaching leads to the following thought: All are told to believe the Gospel, but if you are not one of the elect, you will be damned if you do (believe) and also if you don't.

18. How do you react to the rhyme? Though this rhyme is written in fun, it expresses serious frustration. How have questions of God's will caused frustration for you? for family members?

Christ the Savior

19. In Question 3 you listed examples of God's attitude in the matter of predestination. Now read 1 Peter 1:2. How does this passage describe God's intentions?

20. What person is central to Peter's statements about salvation in 1 Peter 1:2–7 and 11? Explain.

17

21. Consult the apostle's words in 1 Peter 1:19–20; 3:18. For whom did God act and how did He act? See 2 Corinthians 5:15, 19. How does this fulfill God's will, expressed in 1 Timothy 2:4 and 2 Peter 3:9?

22. How is the truth about Jesus applied in 1 Peter 1:10–12 and 23–25?

23. In what ways does God carry out His intentions for predestination according to 1 Peter 1:2–9 and 19? See also John 10:27–29.

24. What reactions from believers are indicated in 1 Peter 1:3, 6, 8?

Christ the Focus of Faith

25. The Lutheran Confessions call Christ "the Book of Life" in which all who shall be eternally saved are inscribed and in which Christians are to look for knowledge of their election. Find two examples of this title in the Appendix of Lutheran Teaching toward the back of this book, and ponder the meaning of it. Also read John 1:1 and write your reflections below.

26. How does the focus of faith in Christ help us consider the issue of whether there is a predestination to eternal death?

27. How is Lorenzo Dow's rhyme at the beginning of this session a distortion of the scriptural doctrine of election?

28. Fatalism discourages people from living by faith because in fatalism the things we do make no difference in the end. Some people connect this thought with predestination by arguing, "Why should I make use of Baptism or Absolution, or even believe and repent at all, if I am guaranteed to be saved no matter what happens in my life?" Discuss this question. Consult 1 Peter 1:8–9; 3:21; Acts 2:38 to see whether Peter urged his hearers to have a fatalistic attitude.

29. In what ways is the Christ-centered focus of faith and of election important for the whole Christian church? Look at 1 Peter 1:1–3, 10–12; 2:9; Ephesians 1:1–10, 15–18, 22–23. Are these truths useful for establishing church membership by determining who is elect and who has faith?

30. God's election involves His foreknowledge (1 Peter 1:2). Why would this fact be comforting to Peter's readers, who were suffering persecution and tribulation?

Living Hope in Christ

31. Notice the characteristics of life in Christ that are mentioned in 1 Peter 1:3, 6, 8, and 13 (it is surprising what is coupled with the experience of grief!). Write them below.

Comparisons

Christians state different reasons why God predestines, or elects, someone to salvation. This issue sparked controversy in the fifth century when a monk named Pelagius argued that people had the power to overcome sin and save themselves. St. Augustine, in response, emphasized that people had no power to save themselves and were utterly dependent on God for salvation. He argued that God chose who would be saved and who would be damned. In response, other monks began teaching that the human will had power to choose salvation, but that God also added His grace to help in conversion (Semipelagianism).

In 529 a church council gathered at Orange, France. It rejected the teachings of Pelagius and the Semipelagians and largely restated Augustine's views as compatible with Scripture. However, unlike Augustine, the council concluded that God did not predestine anyone to hell. The different views summarized below still reflect the issues of this early debate.

Double Predestination: This view was emphasized by John Calvin and follows the teaching of Augustine in emphasizing election solely on the basis of grace. Traditional Reformed churches and Particular Baptists hold this teaching. "By the decrees of God, for the manifestation of his glory, some men and angels are predestined unto everlasting life, and others foreordained to everlasting death" (*The Westminster Confession of Faith*, chapter III.III).

In view of faith or obedience: Wesleyans, Free-Will Baptists, and others emphasize the freedom and power of the human will. They teach that God chose to save certain people because He foresaw that they would believe the Gospel or obey His Word.

Unresolved cause of election: Roman Catholics do not explain why God chose the elect, whether by grace, faith, or obedience. They teach that God predestined no one for hell (*Catechism of the Catholic Church*, para. 1037).

Universalism: This view was expressed by the early Christian teacher Origen and has grown popular among Christians influenced by liberalism. It teaches that all people will eventually be saved. Some hold that there may be a time of punishment for the wicked, but no eternal punishment.

The mystery of God's love in Christ: Lutherans assert that God's Word teaches the election of all true believers by His grace in Christ. They also assert that, although the Bible teaches that some people will go to hell, it does not state that God predestined these people to hell. Lutherans do not attempt to solve this paradox since Scripture itself does not resolve it. They emphasize that election is a mystery, which human reason cannot solve.

Point to Remember

He predestined us to be adopted as His sons through Jesus Christ. Ephesians 1:5

To prepare for "Not a Dark Cloud," read 2 Thessalonians 2:13–17.

Not a Dark Cloud

I don't know if we each have a destiny, or if we're all just floating around accidental-like on a breeze, but I, I think maybe it's both. Maybe both is happening at the same time.

—From the film *Forrest Gump.*

At the heart of the film *Forrest Gump* were questions of God's will and the future, which troubled the main characters. For many people, the issue of predestination hangs over their hearts like a dark cloud.

When Dr. C. F. W. Walther's congregation raised questions about predestination, Walther addressed their concerns by showing the connection between predestination and the joy of Christmas. He explained that predestination does not hang over believing Christians as a dark, threatening storm cloud, so that they must always anxiously ask, "Ah, am I also a chosen one?" No, far from being a dark cloud, the doctrine of predestination is much more a brightly shining sun of grace, comfort, and joy, which rises over every person as soon as he has been called by the Gospel and thereby has become a believer (C. F. W. Walther, "Sermon on Predestination," 1881).

32. What can make this doctrine seem like a dark cloud? Has it ever seemed so to you, or to someone you know?

Thank God!

33. What reason for thanksgiving does Paul give in 2 Thessalonians 2:13? Compare this with his reason in 1 Thessalonians 1:2–4.

34. The Word of God takes for granted that one *can* know of one's election. In the following examples, whom do the apostles direct to think

23

of their election: Colossians 1:2; 2 Thessalonians 1:1; Ephesians 1:1–4; 1 Peter 1:1–2?

35. By what means has God chosen to bring about the salvation of the elect (2 Thessalonians 2:13)? How does this help to remove the dark cloud?

36. What should follow from thankful knowledge of one's election (2 Thessalonians 2:15–17)?

37. What do the apostolic teachings have to do with election and its consequences? See 2 Thessalonians 2:15; relate this to Titus 1:1–3 and 2 Timothy 2:8–10.

Through the Gospel

38. Since lost and condemned sinners are in a predicament from which no human resources can help them escape, are they in fact without hope?

39. What is the importance of the Gospel, according to 2 Thessalonians 2:13–14 and 1 Thessalonians 1:4–10? How can this truth be used to dispel the dark cloud of predestination?

40. Why, do you think, was the doctrine of election not set forth to pagans on Mars Hill (Acts 17), but rather to Christian believers (as in Romans 8–11; Ephesians 1; 2 Thessalonians 2; 1 Peter 1)? How might this guide discussion about matters of faith in your personal conversations? in your congregation?

Stand Firm

41. Give examples of how you can show the steadfastness and loyalty called for in 2 Thessalonians 2:15.

42. Discuss how firmness and certainty about the Christian teaching of election can be maintained. Consider the benefit mentioned in 1 Peter 1:3–5 and the use of prayers such as 1 Thessalonians 3:11–13 and 2 Thessalonians 2:16–17 to implore the Lord that it come to pass in your life as well as in the lives of your fellow believers.

Comparisons

The strict Calvinism of New England Puritans and other Reformed churches made the subject of predestination a matter of grave fear and uncertainty during the First Great Awakening in America (1726–60). As a result, more and more preachers focused on a personal experience of salvation and a life of obedience as ways to tell whether one was truly chosen by God. In time these proofs of experience and obedience became the reasons people believed that God chose some for salvation but not others. These proofs were features of the Second Great Awakening (1800–1830) and have remained key features of revivalism.

Religious awakenings and revivalism affected Lutherans in America, sparking much debate about church practice. Although Lutherans were divided by the topic of election during the Predestination Controversy of the 1880s, they did not dramatically change their teaching, as did the Reformed. Today, Lutherans continue to emphasize that election is a mystery of God. They focus on God's promises in Christ and the means of grace.

Point to Remember

We ought always to thank God for you, brothers loved by the Lord, because from the beginning God chose you to be saved. 2 Thessalonians 2:13

To prepare for "By Grace Alone," read 2 Timothy 1:1–13.

By Grace Alone

"But Halvor, tell me, what is really your opinion about this election or predestination business, or whatever you call it?"
"Oh, to tell you the truth, I haven't been lying awake nights thinking about it. It's a very difficult and involved affair, perhaps a mystery best left alone by mortals. But in my own simple way I am inclined to believe what a certain wise man has said, namely, that one can't expect to be elected unless he agrees to be a candidate."

—From *Halvor,* by Peer Strømme.

Many people, like Halvor Helgeson, the Norwegian pastor in this story, have considered how they could become elected as possessors of eternal life. The same idea appears in another story, *Hellbent for Election*, in which a man condemned to hell finally is elected to become a resident of heaven, after he turns toward the Lord in repentance.

43. In view of your study of Scripture, are these helpful ways of thinking about election?

Not Because of Works

44. How is God's electing purpose described in Ephesians 1:4, 9, 11; Romans 8:28–29; 2 Timothy 1:9?

45. In 2 Timothy 1:9 how is the divine purpose related to our works? Ponder the significance of Acts 13:48.

46. How does election underscore the truth that salvation is by grace alone? Look at Ephesians 1:5–9; Romans 11:5–6; 2 Timothy 1:9.

47. How does the knowledge of election give us the spirit called for in 2 Timothy 1:7 and the attitude urged in verses 8 and 12?

48. Read 2 Timothy 1:8. Of what might Timothy be ashamed in his Christian life and work? Why need he not be ashamed? Consider his lack of confidence alluded to in 1 Corinthians 16:10–11 and 1 Timothy 4:12. Can you personally relate to such problems?

49. In 2 Timothy 1:3–5, 9–11 Paul mentions how God brought about His purpose of predestination. Make note of these ways.

50. What work of Christ is proclaimed in the Gospel according to 2 Timothy 1:10?

51. Paul's themes in 2 Timothy 1 have implications for the whole people of God. Look at verses 3–5 and 13 and reflect on these themes in your life.

Gospel Grace

52. When an elderly pious woman heard of some arguments going on about predestination, she said, "Ah, I have long settled that point in my own mind. For if God had not chosen me long before I was born, I am sure He would have seen nothing in me that would lead Him to choose me afterward." Do you agree or disagree? Why?

53. Someone explained the doctrine of election in this way: "The Lord is always voting for a man, and the devil is always voting against him. Then the man himself votes, and that breaks the tie!" Do you agree? Why or why not?

54. Someone may state, "We surely do need God's grace and couldn't be saved without it. But I know that we have to do our part too." How might you respond?

55. 2 Thessalonians 2:14 and 2 Timothy 1:9 speak of how the Lord called the elect through the Gospel. Can such a call to believe and receive grace be extended to *all* people?

He Is Able

56. 2 Timothy 1:12 teaches that God is able to guard and keep us in our relationship with Him until the Last Day. Romans 14:4; 16:25; and other passages give the same assurance. Some think that this promise to preserve people in the faith is the meaning and comfort of election—

namely, that God has determined to preserve the faith *of all those who turn to Him* and is able to keep them unto the end. Is this view correct?

57. Are there situations in your life when you need reminders of God's support and action for you? Discuss.

Comparisons

The following illustrates how different groups might respond to the question "How do you know you are going to heaven?"

Typical response: I am a good person.
Liberal: Heaven is a state of mind.
Eastern Orthodox: I pray, have faith, and do good works. I belong to the true church.
Roman Catholic: I can't be sure I'm going to heaven because that would be prideful. But I belong to the true church.
Calvinist/Reformed: God chose me by grace to believe His Word and live according to it. (Proofs of faith.)
Revivalist: I have accepted Jesus Christ as my personal Savior. (Personal commitment.)
Lutheran: The Holy Spirit has called me by the Gospel of Jesus Christ through Baptism and God's Word. (Means of grace.)

Point to Remember

[God] has saved us and called us to a holy life—not because of anything we have done but because of His own purpose and grace. 2 Timothy 1:9

To prepare for "Predestination by Lamplight," read Romans 8:28–39.

Predestination by Lamplight

Moreover, who knows whether I am elected to salvation?
Answer: Look at the words, I beseech you, to determine how and of
whom He is speaking. "God so loved the world," and "that whosoever
believeth in Him." Now, the "world" does not mean Saints Peter and
Paul alone but the entire human race, all together. And no one is here
excluded. God's Son was given for all. All should believe, and all who do
believe should not perish, etc. Take hold of your own nose, I beseech
you, to determine whether you are not a human being (that is, part of the
world) and, like any other man, belong to the number of those comprised
by the word "all."

—From *What Luther Says,* §1859, compiled by Ewald Plass, © 1959 CPH.

Luther's remark shows how the Word of God can be used to guide our teaching and understanding of election and salvation. This is lamplight shining on our path (and in this case, on our nose).

58. In your own words, what is Luther saying to those who think that there is no Savior for him or her because they do not know if they are elected?

We Know

59. Read Romans 8:38–39. Of what is Paul convinced? Relate this conviction to the sure knowledge of verse 28.

60. What brings about such knowledge and conviction? Consult Psalm 119:105, 130; 2 Corinthians 1:20; Titus 1:1–3; Acts 28:23; John 8:31–32; Romans 1:16; 10:17.

61. What light does Romans 8:29 shed on the intention of divine election?

62. Like 1 Peter 1:2, Romans 8:29 teaches that predestination involves *foreknowledge*. What light does 2 Thessalonians 2:13 shed on the relationship of predestination, foreknowledge, and saving faith? See also Galatians 4:9.

63. Examine Romans 8:28–39. How is election related to justification? to expectation of God's unfailing love in all circumstances? to victory over difficulties?

64. Is Paul's view of predestinated salvation Christ-centered? Note his wording in Romans 8:29, 32, 34–35, 37–39.

Light for Faith

65. How does the Word of God show the connection between election and other Christian teachings, such as damnation, saving faith, grace, means of grace, the warning and the comfort of the Word of truth, the church?

66. What promises are given to the elect in Matthew 24:22, 24, 31; Mark 13:27; Luke 18:7?

67. How is God's control of all outcomes related to the decisions people make? Consult Proverbs 20:24; Ephesians 1:11; James 4:13–15; 1 Corinthians 16:7; Proverbs 16:9. How does predestination to salvation fit into this picture?

Light for Living

Mark Twain's *Huckleberry Finn* describes a sermon preached to feuding families who keep their guns handy. "Everybody said it was a good sermon," Huck notes, "and they all talked it over going home, and had such a powerful lot to say about faith and good works and free grace and preforeordestination, and I don't know what all, that it did seem to me to be one of the roughest Sundays I had run across yet." Twain's suggestion that the topic of predestination has no usefulness at all for the way people live is intended as an amusing comment. This reaction is an exact match for the attitudes of many people.

68. Discuss this point. *Does* the teaching of predestination promote Christian sanctification, or not? Consider Colossians 3:12–14.

69. Why does God let Christians suffer for their faith?

70. How do you "make your . . . election sure" (2 Peter 1:10)?

Point to Remember

Those He predestined, He also called; those He called, He also justified; those He justified, He also glorified. Romans 8:30

Leader Guide

This guide is provided as a "safety net," a place to turn for help in answering questions and for enriching discussion. It will not answer every question raised in your class. Please read it, along with the questions, before class. Consult it in class only after exploring the Bible references and discussing what they teach. Please note the different abilities of your class members. Some will easily find the Bible passages listed in this study; others will struggle. To make participation easier, team up members of the class. For example, if a question asks you to look up several passages, assign one passage to one group, the second to another, and so on. Divide the work! Let participants present the answers they discover.

Each topic is divided into four easy-to-use sections.

Focus introduces key concepts that will be discovered.

Inform guides the participants into Scripture to uncover truths concerning a doctrine.

Connect enables participants to apply what is learned in Scripture to their lives and provides them an opportunity to formulate and articulate a defense of a key doctrine.

Vision provides participants with practical suggestions for extending the theme of the lesson out of the classroom and into the world.

Also take note of the "Comparisons" section at the end of each lesson. The editor has drawn this material from the official confessional documents and historical works of the various denominations. The passages describe and compare the denominations so that students can see how Lutherans differ from other Christians and also see how all Christians share many of the same beliefs and practices. The passages are not polemical.

Chosen from Eternity

Objectives

By the power of the Holy Spirit working through God's Word, participants will (1) describe the nature and intended purpose of the election of grace; (2) understand the divine concern for sinners shown in it; and (3) give thanks for the blessing of election.

Opening Worship

To introduce the topic for the whole study, sing "Alleluia! Let Praises Ring" (*LW* 437; *TLH* 23). Ask participants to point out the references to election in this hymn.

Focus

Read the opening paragraphs (or sing the stanza if hymnals are available), and invite responses to the question. Any answers given may be kept in mind for later comment when portions of the study apply.

1. *Election* refers to choosing; *predestination* means determining something beforehand.

2. Some may feel that this teaching speaks of people as though they were puppets of a supernatural puppet-master, that it denies the dignity of human beings as decision-makers, or that it means some people are predestined to hell. There may be other concerns as well.

Chosen (Inform)

3. God's election of Israel as the chosen nation shows His love and amazing grace and generosity, not basing His choice on the size of their population or on their righteousness (Deuteronomy 7:6–8; 9:4–6). His election of Paul (Acts 9:15) and the Twelve (Luke 6:13) to apostleship and of Jesus to be the Messiah (Luke 23:35; 1 Peter 1:19–20; 2:4) shows His wise, serious intention to appoint some persons to special experiences and purposes. The Christian church as a whole is a chosen people

(1 Peter 2:9), a New Testament Israel dear to God. The election of individuals to be saved believers (examples are Colossians 3:12; James 2:5; and 1 Corinthians 1:28–29) expresses the same love and appointing purpose.

4. First, He chose them to be holy and blameless in His sight. They are holy and blameless by forgiveness of their sins and justification, which declares them righteous. This purpose will involve the creation of justifying faith (Romans 3:28). They are also holy by the life-sanctifying work of the Holy Spirit, which is given to all who have justifying faith, so that their doing of good works is included in their predestination (Galatians 3:11–14; Ephesians 2:8–10).

Second, He chose them to be adopted as His sons, graciously accepted by Him as their Father. (It may be helpful to point out that "God" in Scripture passages usually refers to God the Father.)

5. Women are not excluded from the family of God (Galatians 3:26–28). The blessing is called sonship to emphasize the assurance of rights of inheritance, as Galatians 3:29 and 4:7 show. In ancient Israel daughters did not always have the inheritance rights that sons had. For example, see Numbers 27:1–8. But Paul calls believing women "sons" to indicate that they can be sure of a son's right when it comes to receiving the heavenly inheritance.

6. It was before creation, before the adoptees existed.

7. It was an act of His love (verse 5), His freely given grace (verse 6). Furthermore, He chose the elect "in Him" (verse 4)—that is, in Christ—because of His redemptive work and merits.

8. The other persons showed their oneness with the Father by cooperating in carrying out His election decision. The Son's work of atonement is applied for the redemption of the elect (Ephesians 1:5–8), and He acts as their head as they find their hope in Him (verses 10–13). The Holy Spirit brings about that hope and faith and gives them a guarantee of the heavenly inheritance by beginning the new life in them (verses 13–14; 1 Corinthians 12:3; Acts 13:48).

9. God, in the first place, blesses the elect by declaring and bringing about their redemption, and Paul calls upon them to join him in blessing and praising God in grateful response for His glorious grace.

Chosen to What? (Connect)

10. Recall Question 4 regarding the benefits for which we have been chosen: forgiveness, holiness, the work of the Spirit, faith, and adoption. We will want to appreciate and use these realities.

11. Ephesians 2:1 teaches that the unconverted are dead in sin. Since the dead cannot raise themselves, human beings *cannot* use their will to turn to God or believe the Gospel. The origin of turning and believing is in God, who predestines it.

12. Answers will vary. Remind participants that God has predestined more than the mere possibility of salvation. In love, He chooses people. No doubt, people will abuse God's grace. But that doesn't mean we should hide or obscure His message of love. In fact, what message is more likely to inspire faithfulness and good works!

13. No, the predestination of salvation of people also includes the foreordaining of how it is to come to pass.

14. On the contrary, the act of divine election shows how concerned God is about the elect one.

15. This proposal is always attractive to some. But Paul treats the teaching as an important, valuable truth for which we praise God. It belongs to "the whole will of God," which ought to be proclaimed for the building up of Christians (Acts 20:27, 32). What could be more important than the Lord's provision for eternal life with Him?

Blessed! (Vision)

16. Discuss the mutual pattern of blessing in God's relationship with His people, and encourage the participants to give expressions of thankful love and heartfelt praise.

17. Answers will vary. Encourage participants to follow the apostle's example in praise and to revel in the positive, encouraging attitude he expresses toward fellow believers.

For Jesus' Sake

Objectives

By the power of the Holy Spirit working through God's Word, participants will (1) recognize the connection between faith in Christ and divine election to eternal life; (2) appreciate how important a Christ-centered approach to election is for the Christian church; and (3) rejoice in the living hope that comes from the fact of divine election.

Opening Worship

To introduce the topic, sing "Hail, O Once Rejected Jesus" (*LW* 284; *TLH* 367).

Focus

18. Have someone read the paragraph. Dow's rhyme may need some further explanation. Participants can be invited to make positive or negative reactions to it. It will be evaluated later in the study.

Christ the Savior (Inform)

19. In predestination God has appointed the elect persons for obedience to Him, that is, a healing of hostile, disobedient sinners so they can trust and serve Him. They are also appointed for an application of Jesus' atoning blood for justification and its results. These blessings come about through the sanctifying work of the Holy Spirit.

20. These verses point to Jesus Christ as Lord, to His atoning sacrifice.

21. He is the Lamb sacrificed for the unrighteous, to reconcile them to God (1 Peter 1:19–20; 3:18; look at John 1:29). He died for the whole world (2 Corinthians 5:15, 19), for God wants all to be saved (1 Timothy 2:4; 2 Peter 3:9). Election was a special act of God's grace by which He determined to apply the atoning blood of Jesus to the elect.

22. According to these verses, it is the work of the Spirit of Christ to reveal the saving message of Christ's atonement through predictions

of the atonement by Old Testament prophets and apostolic preaching about the atonement after it took place. This revelation is the Word of the Gospel, which regenerates sinners with the new life of hope, in which verse 3 exalts.

23. God has determined to bring about the healing and restoration of the elect by applying to them the atonement Jesus was appointed to make for all mankind and bringing them to faith in Him as their Redeemer (1 Peter 1:2–9, 19). He will shield and guard them in faith until the culmination of their salvation (verses 4–5). Thus the Good Shepherd promises that no one can snatch them out of His hand (John 10:27–29). These predestined actions will come to pass in the lives of Christians.

24. Their reactions are unending joy, praise, glorifying, and love for Christ.

Christ the Focus of Faith (Connect)

25. See the entries from *Concordia Triglotta* (pp. 833, 1091–93) toward the back of this study (pp. 52–54). Those who trust in Christ look to Him for knowledge of their election. In their faith in Him they see their election being carried out. The more they gaze at Him and His redemption, the more surely they recognize their election. He is the Word of God (John 1:1), in which the Father expresses love for His creatures and which His people can hear and read with endless pleasure.

26. In His universal grace God has predestined no one to damnation. Christ died for all, and when the elect are brought to faith, they realize that an atonement for all includes atonement for them and rejoice in that fact. Why, then, has the loving God not elected all people to be justified by faith? Many have puzzled over this question. But it is never answered in His Word and so during this life must remain among the unsearchable judgments of God (Romans 11:33).

27. In itself the teaching of particular election is correct. All who are predestined to salvation will be glorified (Romans 8:30); yet some people will receive everlasting punishment (Matthew 25:46). The predicament described in Lorenzo Dow's rhyme will not actually arise: no one will come to an abiding faith in Christ as Savior and yet be denied eternal life because of not being one of the elect. Those who come to such a faith do so because they are elected to do so (Romans 8:30; Acts 13:48) and because of the work of the Holy Spirit through God's Word.

28. The election to salvation is a predestination to the means of conferring grace (Word, Absolution, and Sacraments) and the means of

40

receiving repentant faith. One's salvation comes about in the course of time. Peter taught nothing else but this.

29. Election in Christ and faith in Christ are not merely isolated, independent experiences of individuals. For example, Peter and his readers could rejoice together in their common experience of Christ's benefits, God's electing love, and their union in the elect community of the Christian church. The Old Testament prophets and the New Testament believers were united in their Christ-centered focus. In Ephesians 1 Paul also refers to this shared focus on Christ as Redeemer, Lord, and Head and the love for the saints, who are aware of the eternal riches they all share. The doctrine of predestination helps them to regard each other as "brothers loved by the Lord" (2 Thessalonians 2:13).

Nevertheless, it would be a mistake to attempt to base membership lists on determination of who is elect or has faith. A Christian can know his or her own faith and election and relation to Christ. A Christian may express confidence or encouragement about another person's confession of the Gospel (e.g., 1 Thessalonians 1:4). But Christians cannot know the hearts of others with certainty. Only the Lord has infallible knowledge of His seal on those who are His, for "the LORD does not look at the things man looks at. Man looks at the outward appearance, but the LORD looks at the heart" (1 Samuel 16:7; see also 2 Timothy 2:19). In the church we recognize each one's confession of Christ and in love regard it as genuine unless the hypocrisy of a "brother's" confession becomes clear (as in 1 Corinthians 5).

30. God's foreknowledge of the elect should be exceedingly comforting to them in their sufferings and tribulations of persecution. Their troubles have never been unknown to Him or beyond His power or concern. He knew they would play a role in the demonstration, exercise, and maintaining of their saving faith (1 Peter 1:5–9). Believers can be sure that His purposes for them are far older than their present troubles, extending back before creation.

Living Hope in Christ (Vision)

31. A magnificent vision of the life purposed and predestined by God for His people hopefully will arise from meditation on these verses—praise, living hope, joy coupled with grief (ponder how this can be), love for Christ without yet seeing Him, joy so great it cannot fully be expressed, readiness, and self-control.

Not a Dark Cloud

Objectives

By the power of the Holy Spirit working through God's Word, participants will (1) describe the biblical teaching that the elect can know that they are chosen; (2) confess that God's people find assurance of forgiveness and election through the means of grace; and (3) live in the steadfastness that comes from belief in election.

Opening Worship

To introduce the theme of thankfulness, sing "Baptized into Your Name Most Holy" (*LW* 224; *TLH* 298). The connection made between election and Baptism is worth noting, in view of Question 34 below.

Focus

Have a volunteer read the opening paragraphs and go on to the question.

32. This is an age-old concern in the church: Only some persons are predestined to eternal life. The names of these elect are not spelled out in Scripture. Therefore an individual may well wonder: "Am I one of them?" (Editor's note: When I was in college, my friend Jim went through a great personal struggle over the doctrine of election. He carefully read various opinions on the topic but was not able to "figure it out." At one point, he locked himself in his dorm room and wouldn't talk with any of us for three days. Eventually, He received God's peace concerning this topic. Always remember that this teaching is more than an intellectual problem. It remains a mystery of God's grace. Have patience with those who struggle to understand.)

Thank God! (Inform)

33. In both 2 Thessalonians 2:13 and 1 Thessalonians 1:2–4 Paul expresses thanks for the election of the Thessalonian Christians.

34. It is a recurring theme in their correspondence; they direct the Colossians, the Thessalonians, the Ephesians, and the Christians of Asia Minor (Pontus, Galatia, Cappadocia, Asia, Bithynia) to think of their election.

35. He has predestined them to be saved by means of the Spirit's sanctifying work and by means of faith in the truth. Review the answer to Question 4 on what is included in making one holy. There need be no dark cloud of doubt for a child of God about whether he is elect. If one is a believer in Christ, he or she may confidently trace faith, justification, and renewal back to God's election.

36. After speaking of thankful recognition of election, Paul says that it follows ("So then") that they should stand firm in all the apostolic teaching and with God's help be encouraged and strengthened in good words and works. They will know that they are living in the life to which God has ordained them and are glad of it.

37. The apostolic teachings emphasized in 2 Thessalonians 2:15 give vital instruction to God's people about election, the Savior, the faith indispensably connected with election, and the life into which it brings them. In order to carry out the purposes of election God has entrusted apostles such as Paul with proclaiming His wholesome and illuminating Word, so that by it the hearers may be brought to faith and reconciliation with Him and be fully guided in living in it throughout their lives. Titus 1:1–3 is one place where Paul speaks of this task, and in 2 Timothy 2:10 he says that he faithfully endures much to serve the elect.

Through the Gospel (Connect)

38. No, there is help coming from outside of them—from God, who elects and calls to salvation and glory through a Gospel call. His grace gives good hope (2 Thessalonians 2:16).

39. The elect are predestined to be saved through faith in the truth, and this saving truth is stated in the Gospel, by which they are called (or summoned) to receive the eternal glory Christ has gained for them (2 Thessalonians 2:13–14). In 1 Thessalonians 1:4–10 Paul told the Thessalonian Christians that their election was knowable from their welcome of the Gospel message he brought to them and its effect in their lives. The dark cloud of predestination is dispelled and turned to sunshine when they read Christ as the Book of Life and rejoice in the Savior, in whom God has brought them to trust.

40. Human beings first come to faith, and in that faith they find certainty that they have been elected by God to receive His blessings. Pagans, as people who do not yet have faith, are not in a position to make use of the doctrine of election. The doctrine of election is typically a doctrine to discuss with those who are mature in faith.

Stand Firm (Vision)

41. Answers will vary according to experience.

42. As part of the fulfillment of predestination, God will guard and keep the believer in the state of grace until the entrance into the heavenly inheritance (1 Peter 1:3–5). Even if an elect person temporarily falls from grace, God will restore that person before death. This happened to some of the Galatians (Galatians 5:4).

God's fulfillment of His predestination of individuals will include bringing about prayers in their lives like those in 1 Thessalonians 3 and 2 Thessalonians 2 for preservation in grace and continuance in it. He will answer these prayers by leading His children finally into life eternal.

By Grace Alone

Objectives

By the power of the Holy Spirit working through God's Word, participants will (1) recognize the true causes of election; (2) confess joyfully God's saving power and grace; and (3) apply the implications of the election of grace for themselves and the whole Christian church.

Opening Worship

To introduce the topic, sing "By Grace I'm Saved" (*LW* 351; *TLH* 373).

Focus

43. Read the paragraph and ask the question. Answers will vary. Of course, we don't choose to be candidates of election. God calls us by grace through faith in Christ.

Not Because of Works (Inform)

44. God's purpose of good pleasure toward the elect was centered in Christ, and He chose us in Him (Ephesians 1:4, 9, 11). The elect have been called in accordance with this purpose and have also been justified and glorified (Romans 8:28–29). A key and eternal purpose is to cause us to lead a holy life (2 Timothy 1:9).

45. God's saving purpose is not founded upon our works at all but was prior to the beginning of time and all the works done in time. Election was the application to us of grace, God's favor, in Christ the Redeemer. A holy life of works is certainly God's purpose for us and is the way in which it is realized in us. But the purpose is before the works, and not vice versa. Even the saving faith active in works was not the cause of election or appointment to salvation, but was the result of it, as Acts 13:48 tells us. Review Question 7 on the only causes of election revealed in Scripture.

46. God chose the elect by His good pleasure and grace, the same principle by which He forgives sinners for Jesus' sake (Ephesians 1:5–9). In Ephesians Paul goes on to stress that God's grace is His kindness, not based on our works (2:7–9). Romans 11:5–6 says that in Israel, while some are hardened and lost, there is still a remnant chosen by grace, and if it is by grace, it cannot be by works. According to 2 Timothy 1:9 the predestinating purpose was before any good works and led to the doing of the works.

47. 2 Timothy 1:7 calls for a spirit of power, of love, and of self-discipline. If you know that God has elected you to be Christ's follower, you are aware that He wills to give you this spirit and will help you express it and grow in the use of it. The attitude of being willing to suffer and endure opposition and losses for the sake of the Gospel (verses 8 and 12) stems from the conviction that the Lord has power to guard and keep those whom He has chosen through all difficulties until the Last Day and in fact uses that power to enable us to suffer all for Him.

48. Timothy might be ashamed of being the spokesman of a message unpopular in his society, or of being associated with a religious "jailbird" (Paul in prison). He seems to have fear (1 Corinthians 16:10–11) and belittling criticism directed at him (1 Timothy 4:12). But no one who is called by a gracious, predestinating purpose of an all-powerful God needs to be ashamed of the Gospel. Paul commends to Timothy the good example of Onesiphorus, who had a clear vision of God's purpose (2 Timothy 1:16–18). Invite the participants to find themselves in this picture.

49. God has saved us by the work of Christ, the death-conquering Savior. He appointed Paul and others to be heralds of this work, called us through their Gospel message, heard and answered the prayers of Christians for each other, and provided for the passing of faith from one heart to another—through instruction in His Word. (2 Timothy 3:15–17 tells what happened in Timothy's life.)

The teaching work of Paul and the other apostles is part of the carrying out of God's gracious purpose and is to be steadfastly maintained as the pattern of sound teaching in the church. Review Question 36. The apostolic teaching should be handled with faith and love in Christ, used not just to win arguments but with sincere concern to promote sound teaching in every way.

50. The crucified and risen Savior has removed the curse of death by His atonement for sin, and the Gospel promises eternal life and glorious immortality to all who put their trust in Him. The application of this

life-giving grace through the Gospel of Christ was predestined for the elect before the beginning of time.

51. The scope of thankfulness and mutual love extends to all in whom God's gracious predestinating purpose is carried out. This is the whole people of God, including Paul's believing, God-serving forefathers, Timothy in tears of love, Paul longing for the joy of Timothy's presence, Timothy's pious mother and grandmother, and all who are blessed with the pattern of sound teaching.

Gospel Grace (Connect)

52. Her thinking is right on target, in accord with the fact that the election of grace is not based on our works. Though she was pious like Lois and Eunice in 2 Timothy 1, she also recognized her unworthiness before God. Election by grace happens neither because God sees that any good works have been done, nor because He foresees that they will be done in time to come.

53. The unconverted man cannot vote for his conversion and for the Gospel. He is dead in sin (Ephesians 2:1) and does not accept the things that come from the Spirit (1 Corinthians 2:14). This dreadful condition has been called the "bondage of the will."

54. Those who are in the darkness of unbelief cannot "do our part" to come to faith. God must turn on the light in us (2 Corinthians 4:6). Conversion is purely a gift of God.

55. The call to believe in Christ is based on His death for all human beings and is to be spoken to all the world (Matthew 28:19). Many hearers will not respond with faith. But God uses this Gospel call in bringing the elect to faith.

He Is Able (Vision)

56. We can't turn to Him by our own reason and strength. The proposal presented here is another version of the idea in Questions 53 and 54 that the unconverted can come to faith by their own decision, or cooperate in doing it, and election is God's promise to guard the faith of all who do so. But the same objections must be raised. God is indeed able to preserve faith. But He is also able to originate faith, as He has predetermined to do in election. See Luke 1:37; 2 Thessalonians 2:13; John 1:13; Hebrews 12:2.

57. Answers will vary. It is reassuring to realize that God is able to do all that He has promised to do.

Predestination by Lamplight

Objectives

By the power of the Holy Spirit working through God's Word, participants will (1) understand how God's Word sheds light on election and related topics; (2) find comfort and warning in the biblical teaching of predestination; and (3) use the biblical teaching of predestination in living for Christ and serving others.

Opening Worship

Invite someone to read Psalm 119:97–117. Observe that the Word of God is called a lamp in verse 105 and is commended throughout this whole psalm as a guide for all our belief and life. The scope of this, of course, includes the doctrine of election. Offer a prayer.

Focus

Have someone read the opening quote.

58. Luther does not mean that everyone is elect, or that the Bible teaches universalism (Luther never held that). But he is saying to the questioner that there can be no doubt, in the Gospel statements, that Jesus Christ is the Savior who made atonement for all people and that all are invited to believe in Him. Faith, rightly understood, is the personal appropriation of Christ, which says, "If He came for all, He came also for me." Everyone who does come to faith can then contemplate the truth that "God has elected me to be His child and has called me by this Gospel call." This contemplation is done in the lamplight of the Gospel statements.

We Know (Inform)

59. Nothing can separate God's people from His love in Christ Jesus, that is, turn it into hostility and damnation and delete its benefits. This conviction is inextricably connected to Paul's assertion in verse 28 that "we know" that God will work in all things for the ultimate good of

His people. He goes on in the passage to explain that all this flows from His predestination of them for a glorious purpose.

60. What the elect know, or should know, is the truth of God's Word, which is a lamp and a light-giver (Psalm 119:105, 130), filled with God's great "Yes" in Christ (2 Corinthians 1:20) and wonderful promises that serve the faith of the elect (Titus 1:1–3). God's Word is convincing to them (Acts 28:23), leads them to know the truth (John 8:31–32), is the power for salvation, and brings about faith (Romans 1:16; 10:17).

61. The lamplight of Romans 8:29 reveals how the Father bestows predestined sonship (Ephesians 1:5): He conforms the elect to be like His own Son, making them His dear brothers (and, of course, dear brothers of each other).

62. Many have understood this verse to mean that God elected certain persons to salvation on the basis of His foreknowledge of their faith and/or work. But it has already been shown in this study that faith is a result, not a cause, of election (see 2 Thessalonians 2:13). Therefore, Bible teachers have often pointed out that the foreknowledge mentioned in Romans 8:29 is not simply God's awareness of all that ever happens, but rather the knowledge of a loving relationship between persons. Scripture sometimes speaks of this kind of knowledge, as in Galatians 4:9.

63. Justification is part of the fulfillment of the intention of election (Romans 8:30). So is God's unfailing manifestation of love toward His elect as He prepares them for eternal glory (verses 31–36). He treats those who are justified and reconciled to Him as His children and brings good out of evil for them, even out of suffering. They *do* suffer, but they conquer their troubles in various ways, and their eternal destiny is sure.

64. Yes! Christ is the pattern of predestined destiny (29), the basis of redemption (32), the dying, raised, and exalted One, our intercessor (34), the loving Lord (35, 37–39).

Light for Faith (Connect)

65. These are some examples of the integration of doctrines in the light of Scripture, some of which have already been pointed out.

Damnation—There is no predestination to eternal death (1 Timothy 2:4). But the Son of God was predestined to be damned for sinners (1 Peter 1:19–20), and because of this the elect shall escape damnation.

Saving faith—We are predestined *to* it, not predestined *because* of it (2 Thessalonians 2:13).

Grace—Predestination is an election of grace, showing God's loving concern for the salvation of sinners. But it is based on grace alone, not works (2 Timothy 1:9; Romans 11:5–6).

Means of grace—We are elected to be saved through the means of grace (2 Thessalonians 2:13–14).

Warning—The scriptural doctrine of election will disturb people who rely for salvation on works or on something other than the merits of Christ.

Comfort—It assures the elect of their salvation (Romans 8:28–39; John 10:28).

The church—The members of the church are united as beneficiaries of election (1 Peter 1:1–2; Romans 8:29). Election guarantees the survival of the Christian church (Matthew 24:24; 16:18).

The participants can also be asked to look in the Appendix of Lutheran Teaching (pp. 52–54) for statements about using the Word of God for understanding and using the doctrine of election.

66. These verses say that the Lord will bring about justice for His elect who pray to Him (Luke 18:7), watch over them in the last days (Matthew 24:22, 24), and gather together the elect on earth and those in heaven at the second coming (Matthew 24:31; Mark 13:27).

67. God does control all outcomes in the world (Proverbs 20:24). Predestination to salvation is one facet of this (Ephesians 1:11). Human beings can make decisions and plans about many things, and have a free will to do so, but whether these work out or come to pass is subject to His control (see the other passages). But unconverted folks cannot even decide to believe in Christ, to come to Him, to be converted. In spiritual matters they have bondage of the will. Divine predestination pertains to these matters.

Light for Living (Vision)

68. Those who have a grateful knowledge of their election will want to live in the holy life to which they have been predestined. Note what the elect are to put on because they *are* elect (Colossians 3:12–14; the verses following also belong to Paul's discussion).

69. This is all part of the working out of the purpose of election. If we are elected to conformity with the Son of God, we shall share in His sufferings in order that we may also share in His glory (Romans 8:14–18, 29). The refinement and purification that take place in such suffering are

part of the holiness to which we are elected (1 Peter 1:2–7). The way is described in 1 Peter 1:5–9.

70. Peter says that our election is made sure by diligence in good works, productive knowledge of the Lord Jesus, and remembrance of our forgiveness (2 Peter 1:5–9). This statement might seem to mean that good works and a Christian life are the basis of our election and make us qualified for it, or perhaps that election is provisional until we become worthy of it. But these thoughts contradict the theme studied earlier— election is by grace alone.

What should be noted here is that forms of the same Greek word for "making sure" in the original text are applied to "election" (verse 10) and the Word of the prophets about Christ (verse 19). Both of these are certain and true in themselves. But the word refers to a demonstration that something is true and reliable. The prophecy about Christ is demonstrated to be true by the transfiguration (verses 16–18). And our election to faith, to a Christian life, and to eternal glory is demonstrated by living in that life to which we are predestined and expressing the fruit of faith. Thereby, we may grow in the awareness that God is carrying out His purpose of election in us.

If desired, the "examination" in the Student Introduction (p. 5) can be used for summarizing what has been learned.

Appendix of Lutheran Teaching

The Augsburg Confession of 1530

Philip Melanchthon, a lay associate of Dr. Martin Luther, wrote the Augsburg Confession to clarify for Emperor Charles V just what the Lutherans believed. Melanchthon summarized Lutheran teaching from the Bible and addressed the controversies of the day. This confession remains a standard of Lutheran teaching.

Article XVII. Of Christ's Return to Judgment

He will give to the godly and elect eternal life and everlasting joys (*Concordia Triglotta*, p. 51).

The Formula of Concord

The Formula of Concord was adopted in 1580 to deal with certain controversies and to unify the public confession of the Lutheran church. It has two parts: the Epitome (a summary), and the Thorough Declaration (a longer explanation, also called the Solid Declaration).

Article II. Of Free Will

But if a man will not hear preaching nor read God's Word, but despises the Word and congregation of God, and thus dies and perishes in his sins, he neither can comfort himself with God's eternal election nor obtain His mercy; for Christ, in whom we are chosen, offers to all men His grace in the Word and holy Sacraments (Thorough Declaration, *Concordia Triglotta*, p. 903).

Article XI: Of God's Eternal Election

This [predestination of God] is not to be investigated in the secret counsel of God, but to be sought in the Word of God, where it is also revealed.

But the Word of God leads us to Christ, who is the Book of Life, in whom all are written and elected that are to be saved in eternity, as it is written Ephesians 1:4: *He hath chosen us in Him* [Christ] *before the foundation of the world* (Epitome, *Concordia Triglotta*, p. 833).

When any teach the doctrine concerning the gracious election of God to eternal life in such a manner that troubled Christians cannot comfort themselves therewith, but are thereby led to despondency or despair, or the impenitent are strengthened in their wantonness, that such doctrine is treated [wickedly and erroneously] not according to the Word and will of God, but according to reason and the instigation of the cursed Satan. *For*, as the apostle testifies, Rom. 15:4, *whatsoever things were written aforetime were written for our learning, that we, through patience and comfort of the Scriptures, might have hope.* Therefore we reject the following errors:

1. As when it is taught that God is unwilling that all men repent and believe the Gospel.

2. Also, that when God calls us to Himself, He is not in earnest that all men should come to Him.

3. Also, that God is unwilling that every one should be saved, but that some, without regard to their sins, from the mere counsel, purpose, and will of God, are ordained to condemnation so that they cannot be saved.

4. Also, that not only the mercy of God and the most holy merit of Christ, but also in us there is a cause of God's election, on account of which God has elected us to everlasting life (Epitome, *Concordia Triglotta*, p. 837).

The eternal election of God, however, not only foresees and foreknows the salvation of the elect, but is also, from the gracious will and pleasure of God in Christ Jesus, a cause which procures, works, helps, and promotes our salvation and what pertains thereto; and upon this [divine predestination] our salvation is so founded *that the gates of hell cannot prevail against it*, Matt. 16:18 (Thorough Declaration, *Concordia Triglotta*, p. 1065).

By this doctrine and explanation of the eternal and saving choice [predestination] of the elect children of God His own glory is entirely and fully given to God, that in Christ He saves us out of pure [and free] mercy, without any merits or good works of ours, according to the purpose of His will, as it is written Eph. 1:5f.: *Having predestinated us unto the adoption of children by Jesus Christ to Himself, according to the good pleasure of His will, to the praise of the glory of His grace, wherein*

He hath made us accepted in the Beloved. Therefore it is false and wrong [conflicts with the Word of God] when it is taught that not alone the mercy of God and the most holy merit of Christ, but that also in us there is a cause of God's election, on account of which God has chosen us to eternal life. For not only before we had done anything good, but also before we were born, yea, even before the foundations of the world were laid, He elected us in Christ. . . .

Moreover, this doctrine gives no one a cause either for despondency or for a shameless, dissolute life, namely, when men are taught that they must seek eternal election in Christ and His holy Gospel, as in the Book of Life, which excludes no penitent sinner, but beckons and calls all the poor, heavy-laden, and troubled sinners [who are disturbed by the sense of God's wrath], to repentance and the knowledge of their sins and to faith in Christ, and promises the Holy Ghost for purification and renewal, and thus gives the most enduring consolation to all troubled, afflicted men, that they know that their salvation is not placed in their own hands,—for otherwise they would lose it much more easily than was the case with Adam and Eve in paradise, yea, every hour and moment,—but in the gracious election of God, which He has revealed to us in Christ, out of whose hand no man shall pluck us, John 10:28; 2 Timothy 2:19 (Thorough Declaration, *Concordia Triglotta*, pp. 1091–93).

Glossary

election. From the Latin word "to choose." The teaching that God chose to save His people even before He created the world. See *predestination.*

filioque. Literally, "and the Son." This Latin word was added to the Nicene Creed in the West to emphasize that the Holy Spirit proceeds from the Father *and the Son.*

foreknowledge. The teaching that God knows everything before it happens, including who will believe and who will not believe.

Gospel. The message of Christ's death and resurrection for the forgiveness of sins. The Holy Spirit works through the Gospel to create faith and convert people.

grace. Good will or favor shown to someone who does not deserve it. Because of the sacrifice of Christ for our sins, God is gracious toward us.

justification. God declares sinners to be just, or righteous, for Christ's sake; that is, God has imputed or charged our sins to Christ, and He imputes or credits Christ's righteousness to us.

means of grace. The means by which God gives us the forgiveness, life, and salvation won by the death and resurrection of Christ: the Gospel, Baptism, and the Lord's Supper.

polemical. From the Greek word for "battle." The term describes conversation or writing that attacks and refutes.

predestination. The act of God whereby He chose who would be saved in Christ. See *election.*

revivalism. A movement that attempts to assist the conversion of people by stirring up, or "reviving," faith through emotional and persuasive appeals. Revivalism emerged as a method of conversion in American Protestantism. Revivalists emphasize that people need to choose or decide for their own salvation.

sanctification. The spiritual growth that follows justification by grace through faith in Christ.